How to Be a MEDIEVAL KNIGHT

by Nel Yomtov

PEBBLE
a capstone imprint

Pebble is published by Capstone,
1710 Roe Crest Drive, North Mankato, Minnesota 56003
capstonepub.com

Copyright © 2026 by Capstone. All rights reserved. No part of this publication may be reproduced in whole or in part, or stored in a retrieval system, or transmitted in any form or by any means, electronic, mechanical, photocopying, recording, or otherwise, without written permission of the publisher.

Library of Congress Cataloging-in-Publication Data is available on the Library of Congress website.

ISBN: 9798875226861 (hardcover)
ISBN: 9798875234293 (paperback)
ISBN: 9798875234309 (ebook PDF)

Summary: Journey back in time to medieval Europe and become a knight! Learn about the armor, weapons, and tactics of these fierce fighters and find out if you have what it takes to ride into battle as a knight for your kingdom.

Editorial Credits
Editor: Alison Deering; Designer: Bobbie Nuytten; Media Researcher: Svetlana Zhurkin; Production Specialist: Whitney Schaefer

Image Credits
Bridgeman Images: © Look and Learn, 12, Otus/Index, 14, Photo © North Wind Pictures, 11; Getty Images: clu, 21, 26, duncan1890, 8, 23, FXQuadro, 16, Grafissimo, 20, 24, Hein Nouwens, 18, Nastasic, 13, 28, powerofforever, 17, ThePalmer, 27, ZU_09, 7; Newscom: Album/Florilegius, 9; Shutterstock: adolf martinez soler (stone wall), cover and throughout, Anterovium, 15, Burak Erdal, cover (bottom right), jan kranendonk, cover (top), Javier Jaime, 25, Nejron Photo, 29, Pic Media Aus, 19, Yarikart, 5, Yip Po Yu (texture), cover and throughout

Any additional websites and resources referenced in this book are not maintained, authorized, or sponsored by Capstone. All product and company names are trademarks™ or registered® trademarks of their respective holders.

Table of Contents

Introduction
So You Want to Be a Medieval Knight?...................................4

Chapter 1
Are You Tough Enough?........................6

Chapter 2
Tools of the Trade............................... 14

Chapter 3
Off to War!.. 20

Chapter 4
In Times of Peace 26

Test Your Knightly Knowledge 30
Glossary... 31
Index 32
About the Author 32

Words in **bold** are in the glossary.

So You Want to Be a Medieval Knight?

For this job, get ready to journey back in time to medieval Europe, around 1400–1500. Knights were famous warriors who trained hard and fought in battles. They worked for themselves or were hired by kings and wealthy lords to protect and expand their kingdoms.

A life of adventure, fame, and riches awaits you. But in time of war, you will face terrible dangers—and maybe an early death!

Do YOU have what it takes to be a medieval knight?

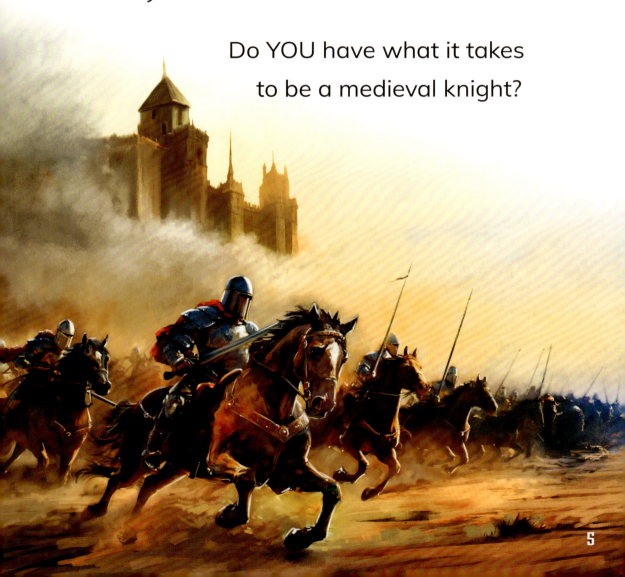

Chapter 1

Are You Tough Enough?

Your chances of becoming a knight will be better if your father is also a knight, or at least a wealthy man. After all, you'll need money for weapons, armor, and horses.

Your training starts at about age seven when you become a **page**. You'll be sent to live at a royal court or the home of a local lord. There you will learn to handle and ride horses. You'll use fake wooden weapons like swords and shields in the games you play with other pages.

As a knight in training, you'll also learn good manners. It's your job to serve the lords and ladies of the house at the dinner table. You'll also care for your lord's clothing and help him dress. If you're lucky, you'll be taught to read and write.

Tip #1: Aim Carefully

Learn to use a type of spear called a **lance**. Holding a fake lance, you sit atop a wooden horse on wheels. Other pages quickly pull the horse toward a target. Carefully aim your weapon and strike!

At age 14, you'll move on to become a **squire**. You'll work under a knight and train with real weapons, such as the lance and sword. You might even practice using the crossbow. You'll clean the knight's weapons and help him dress for battle.

But be warned. Your time as a squire is when your life of danger begins. You'll have to follow your knight onto the battlefield. Are you prepared to pull him to safety if he's hurt? Can you help him back on his horse if he's knocked off? And don't forget to watch out for flying arrows!

By about age 21, you're ready to be made a knight. The religious ceremony is called a **dubbing**. You spend the night before praying to be protected as a future knight.

On the special day, you kneel before a nobleman—or even the king himself! He gives you a gentle tap on the shoulders with a sword. Congratulations—you have been knighted!

Chapter 2

Tools of the Trade

To protect yourself in battle, you'll need a strong suit of armor. Choose the finest **silversmith** in town to make it for you. The suit is made of steel plates held together by laces, straps, and buckles.

The armor covers your entire body. But it weighs only about 45 pounds (20 kilograms). That's less than a large bag of dog food! You'll still be able to move around easily. Under your armor, you wear padded clothing to protect your skin.

Your main weapon is called a longsword. You'll need both hands to use this heavy weapon. It weighs about 4 pounds (1.8 kg) and measures 50 inches (1.3 meters) long.

The longsword is meant to thrust and slash at your foe. It's heavy enough to knock him off his horse. Your young squire may also arm you with a lance, a **mace**, and a **poleax**.

You'll need a strong warhorse to carry you into combat. Your wealth allows you to buy a large, heavy horse called a **destrier**. A destrier has a powerful body and a strong neck. To protect your destrier in battle, you provide it with a suit of armor that covers from the tip of its nose to its tail.

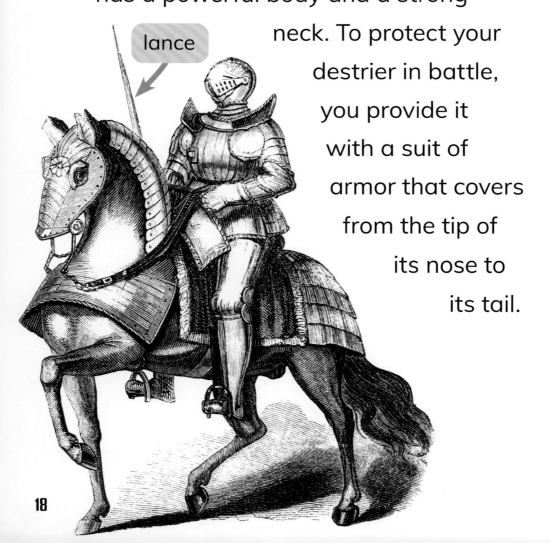

lance

Tip #2: Horseback Tips and Tricks

Train your destrier to make it ready for battle! Teach it to respond to your commands using nudges from your legs. Train it to charge straight toward the enemy. You can also teach it to bite and kick on command.

Chapter 3

Off to War!

Today your king has called for you to fight against an enemy nation. You've prepared for this moment for many years. Are you up to the challenge?

You travel many difficult miles across the countryside into battle. You and hundreds of other knights ride your destriers in the hot sun and pouring rain. Dirt roads have turned into pits of mud.

You travel with your squire and other assistants. They carry many supplies. A wealthy knight like you brings tents, bedding, chests of clothing, and cooking supplies.

You also bring small amounts of food such as bread, fruits, and cooked meat. But you will have to find more food from the countryside or take it from enemies you defeat in combat. You might even have to steal it from villagers along the way.

The day of battle has finally arrived. Fighting begins as enemy archers send a flurry of deadly metal-tipped arrows in your direction. Suddenly, hundreds of horsemen charge at you. You attack their line with your lance. But you're knocked off your horse and must fight hand to hand with an enemy knight!

The sound of men shouting and weapons clanging is deafening. The heat is unbearable inside your suit of armor. You struggle for every breath. The squires do what they can to help the injured, but many of your fellow knights do not survive.

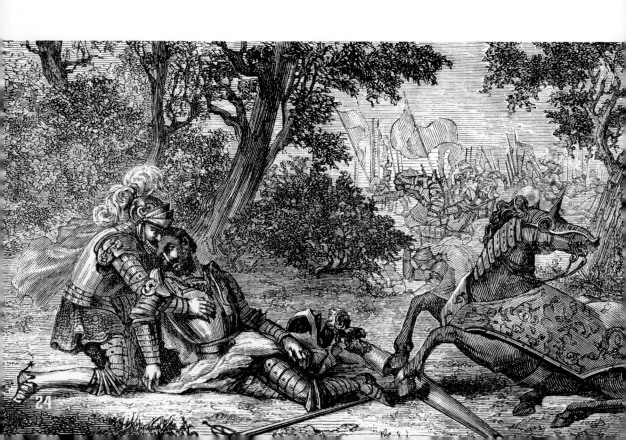

Tip #3: Under Siege

During a **siege**, your army will surround an enemy castle or city. To smash down its walls, learn to use a catapult called a **trebuchet**. This war machine hurls heavy rocks into or over castle walls.

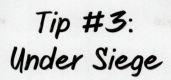

Chapter 4

In Times of Peace

In times of peace, you live a comfortable life. The lord pays you for your services with money or land. You live in a large castle and have many servants. You wear fine clothing.

In your spare time, you like to hunt deer, fox, and rabbits. You train falcons to help you hunt ducks, cranes, and other types of birds. You compete in **tournaments** to sharpen your fighting and horse-riding skills.

Tip #4: Jousting

Sign up for the joust at your town's next tournament! You and an opponent will fight on horseback with lances. This contest is excellent training for a real battle.

As a medieval knight, you are expected to live a life of **chivalry**. This means you must protect the poor, show respect for women, and be generous to others. You are required to serve your lord, your king, and your country in battle. But be warned: If you fail to live a life of chivalry, your knighthood will be taken from you.

Fear not. You've trained hard, fought bravely, and served well. Go forth and be a knight to remember!

Test Your Knightly Knowledge

1. What is your main weapon?
   a. bow and arrow
   b. longsword
   c. mace and poleax

2. What type of horse do you ride into battle?
   a. mustang
   b. quarter pony
   c. destrier

3. What is a joust?
   a. a pretend sports contest fought on horseback
   b. a type of medieval poetry
   c. another name for a spear

4. Living a life of chivalry means to:
   a. be generous and help the poor
   b. pay taxes to your lord and king
   c. wear fine clothing and jewels

5. Which of these is your duty as a squire?
   a. tending your lord's garden
   b. riding into battle with your lord
   c. making your lord's armor

Answers: 1) b, 2) c, 3) a, 4) a, 5) b

If you answered all the questions correctly, the job of medieval knight is yours! If not, take another read through this book and try the test again!

Glossary

chivalry (SHIV-uhl-ree)—a code of noble and polite behavior that was expected of a medieval knight

destrier (DES-treer)—a medieval knight's warhorse

dubbing (DUHB-ing)—a ceremony in which a squire is made a knight

lance (LANS)—a long spear with a pointed metal tip

mace (MACE)—a heavy club with a metal head and spikes

page (PAYJ)—a young boy being trained to be a knight

poleax (POHL-aks)—a battle-ax with a short handle and a hook or spike

siege (SEEJ)—an attack designed to surround a castle or town and cut it off from supplies or help

silversmith (SIL-vur-smith)—a person who makes objects of metal

squire (SKWIRE)—a young man serving as an assistant to a knight before becoming a knight himself

tournament (TOOR-nuh-muhnt)—a fake battle fought for training and entertainment

trebuchet (trehb-u-SHET)—a machine used during a siege for hurling large stones

Index

armor, 6, 14, 15, 18, 24

battles, 10, 14, 20, 21, 22, 24, 25, 27

ceremonies, 12, 13

clothing, 26

horses, 6, 10, 17, 18, 19, 21, 22, 27

jousting, 27

lifestyle, 26, 27

manners, 8, 28

nobility, 4, 6, 8, 13, 20, 26, 28, 29

pages, 6, 9

payment, 26

squires, 10, 17, 21, 24

supplies, 21, 22

tournaments, 27

training, 6, 8

weapons, 6, 9, 10, 16, 17, 22, 24, 25, 27

About the Author

Nel Yomtov is an award-winning author of children's nonfiction books and graphic novels. He specializes in writing about history, current events, biography, architecture, and military history. He has written numerous graphic novels for Capstone, including the recent *The Wright Brothers Take Flight*, *The Christmas Truce of World War I*, and *D-Day Training Turned Deadly: The Exercise Tiger Disaster*. In 2020 he self-published *Baseball 100*, an illustrated book featuring the 100 greatest players in baseball history. Nel lives in the New York City area.